Please Explain "Anxiety" to Me!

Simple Biology and Solutions for Children and Parents

Second Edition

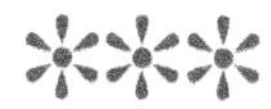

Laurie Zelinger, PhD., RPT-S
&
Jordan Zelinger, M.S. Ed.

Illustrator: Elisa Sabella

Please Explain "Anxiety" To Me : Simple Biology And Solutions For Children And Parents, 2nd Edition.

Illustrations by Elisa Sabella

From the Growing With Love Series
Visit the author online at www.DrZelinger.com

Library of Congress Cataloging-in-Publication Data

Zelinger, Laurie E., 1952-
Please explain "anxiety" to me! : simple biology and solutions for children and parents / Laurie Zelinger, PhD., RPT-S & Jordan Zelinger, M.S. Ed. ; illustrator, Elisa Sabella. -- Second edition.
pages cm -- (Growing with love series)
ISBN 978-1-61599-216-4 (pbk. : alk. paper) -- ISBN 978-1-61599-217-1 (hardcover : alk. paper) --
ISBN 978-1-61599-218-8 (ebook)
1. Anxiety--Juvenile literature. 2. Adjustment (Psychology)--Juvenile literature. 3. Stress (Physiology)--Juvenile literature. I. Zelinger, Jordan, 1987- II. Sabella, Elisa, illustrator. III. Title.
BF575.A6Z45 2014
152.4'6--dc23

2013051371

Distributed by Ingram Book Group (USA/CAN/AUS), Bertram's Books (EU)

Loving Healing Press Inc.
5145 Pontiac Trail
Ann Arbor, MI 48105

www.LHPress.com
info@LHPress.com

Tollfree USA/CAN: 888-761-6268
FAX 734-663-6861

Introduction:

This book is for kids- the kind of kids that are like me when I was little. I was the kind of child who worried a lot, even when I didn't need to. I was always thinking that something bad was going to happen. I worried when I was in school, when I came home from school and especially at bedtime. I worried all the time.

My parents would tell me not to worry, but that didn't work. I kept worrying anyway. I had a great imagination and could get scared over little or big things. I hated worrying and wanted to be just like everyone else. I always had a stomach ache and didn't know why. Then I grew up and learned about "**anxiety**". I found out that anxiety can be good when you have just the right amount. It can give you energy to do your best and help you plan for important things. It also helps you to be sensitive and aware of things around you. But when you have too much anxiety and can't make it go away, that feels really yucky.

This book is for kids who have too much anxiety and want to get rid of some of it. I became a child psychologist because I know what kids think about and I want to help them feel better when they feel worried and scared. I wrote this book because the children I work with said the ideas helped them. If you are a child who also gets anxiety, this book is just for you because everyone who loves you wants you to feel better. Read it over and over again with a grownup you trust. I think you'll like it.

From your friend,
Dr. Laurie, the Feelings Doctor
P.S. I'm a mom too!

Dedication:
to Shirley and Simon Teitelbaum

Once upon a time, before there were people, dinosaurs roamed the earth. Big ones, small ones, fast ones, slow ones, young ones, and old ones.

There wasn't much else around except grass, trees, plants, dirt, rocks, and water.

Sometimes food was hard to find. That's because supermarkets and restaurants weren't invented yet. Of course, this was before farmers too!

Dinosaurs had to work really hard to fill their tummies so they wouldn't go to bed hungry.

Plant eating dinosaurs, called herbivores, found things to eat that grew from the ground, like flowers, grass, and leaves. But meat-eating dinosaurs didn't want plants. They were called carnivores and they only liked to eat other dinosaurs since dinosaurs are made of dinosaur meat. Some dinosaurs even liked to eat both kinds of food.

Smaller species of dinosaurs were scared that meat-eating dinosaurs would eat them. They probably worried a lot because there was danger all around them. They had a really good reason to be afraid!

Whenever a meat-eating dinosaur showed up, a small dinosaur realized he had to do something fast. He probably said to himself, “Hmmm. I have three choices. I can either freeze and stay perfectly still while I stop, look, and listen. Maybe the other dinosaur won’t see me.

Or I can try to run away just as fast as my legs will take me. If those ideas don't work, then I can stay and fight. That's called "freeze, flight, or fight."

The small dinosaurs suddenly needed quick energy so they could move fast. A part of their body called the “sympathetic nervous system” (sim-pa-thet-ik nur-vus-sis-tem) got them ready to rush around.

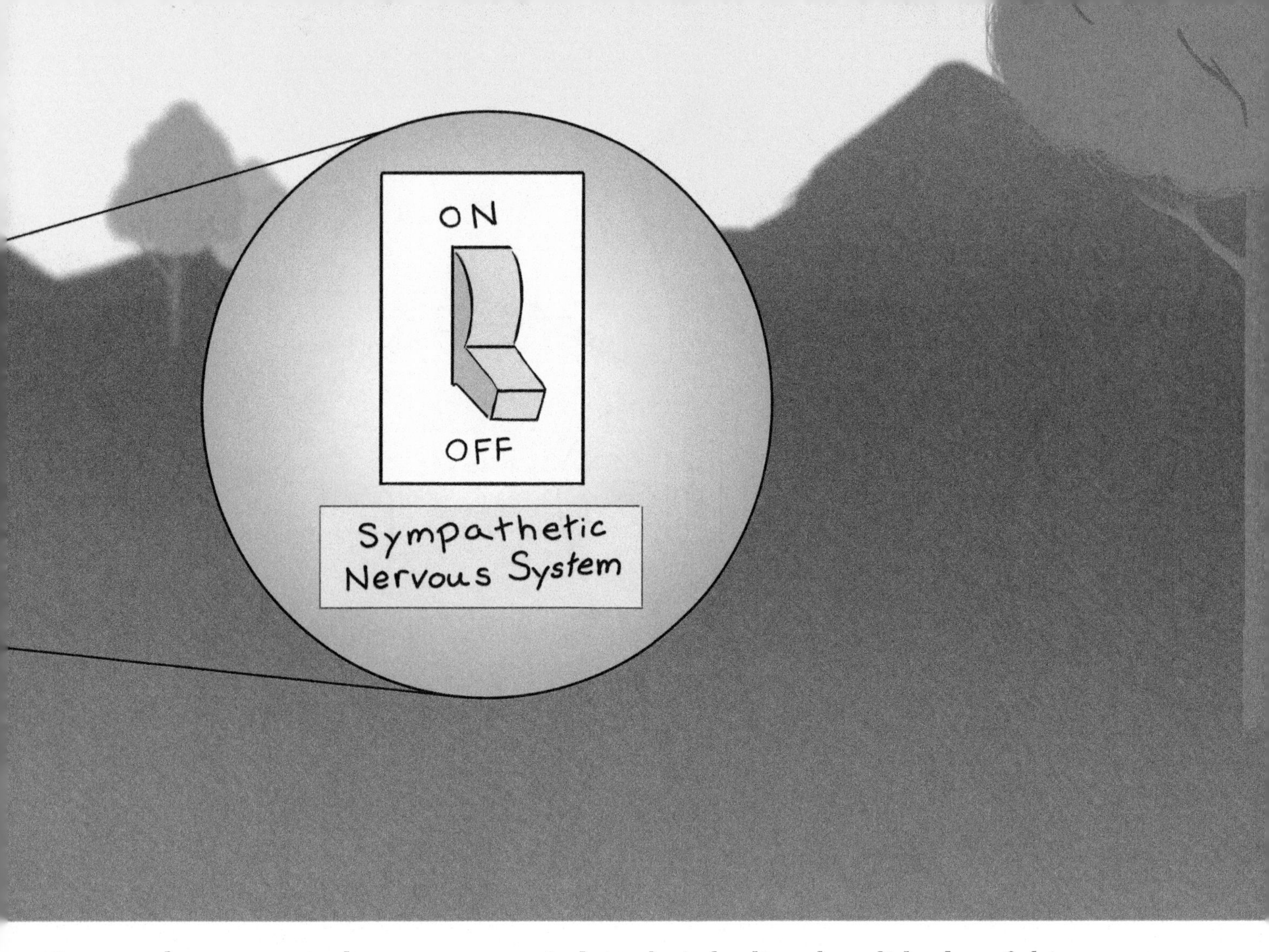

It turned on a pretend *emergency switch* in their bodies that did a lot of things to help them get ready for action when there was real danger.

Their bodies were very busy on the inside getting ready for a big fight or the race to get away. This happened automatically. Sometimes when bodies are working hard on the inside, they can feel tingly, just like when people feel nervous.

But it also shut down some parts of their bodies, like digestion, to save energy in case more was needed later. And it helped their bodies lose extra weight by making a big pile of heavy dinosaur poop right on the ground. Eww! Gross!

The sympathetic nervous system made their hearts beat faster so more blood could rush to their muscles to make them stronger. It helped them breathe faster so they could have more oxygen in their lungs to run faster and longer. Getting ready for an emergency was like exercising on the inside.

The dinosaurs probably got hot and tired from so much stuff going on in their bodies! That happens to people also. We sometimes get hot and sweaty, but when we start to dry off, it makes us cooler.

We have a sympathetic nervous system too, that *switches on* when we think we're in danger. A special tiny part of our brain makes that happen. It's called the amygdala (a-mig'-da-la). It remembers all the other times we became afraid and makes us react the same way. If something scares us, we can feel our heart beat louder and harder, we breathe faster, and our hands might get sweaty. Sometimes we get a headache or dizzy, and we almost always get a stomach ache or a feeling like we're going to throw up. Sometimes we even have a tantrum, a meltdown, or cry.

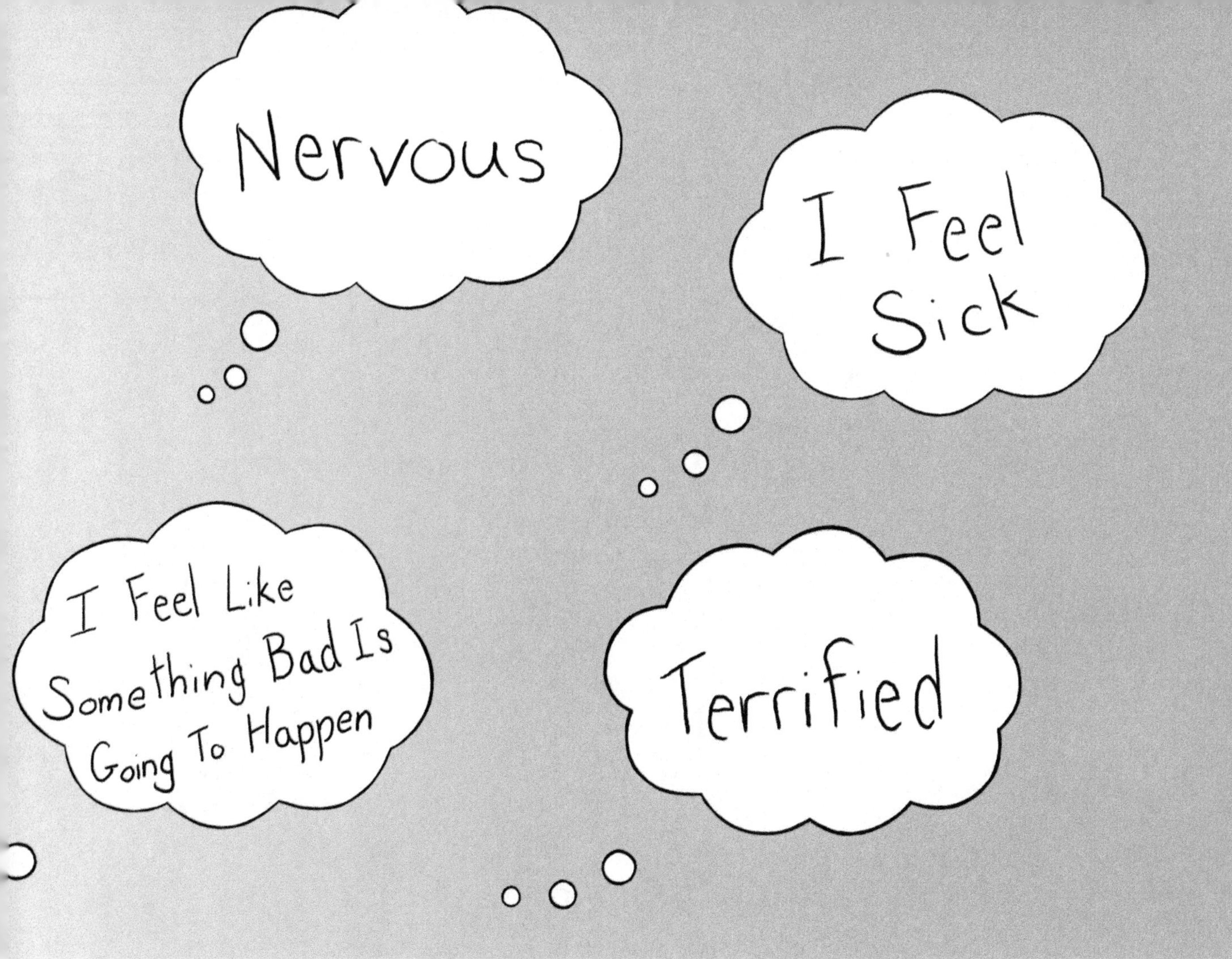

It sometimes feels like something bad is going to happen and then it can be hard to think of anything else or pay attention in school. It's too easy to think of bad things that could happen and too hard to tell ourselves that it won't. Our brains keep our imaginations very busy making every worry even worse.

All of this worrying is usually not a good thing, unless there really is an emergency. Then, of course, our bodies would be ready because our switches are turned on. But sometimes the switch in our body goes on when there isn't a real emergency, and that's the problem. We might feel like there's *real* danger when everything is really okay.

Our brain has tricked us and is making us get ready for an emergency. That feeling of stress is called "anxiety." It can feel pretty yucky when we don't need it or want it. It can feel like something is wrong with our body when we feel this way, but that just means our switch is working! The amygdala flips the switch whenever we feel scared because it can't tell the difference between real danger and danger that we just imagine. Sometimes we even feel like we have to do some silly or annoying things to make it go away and we don't even know why.

Everybody's switch gets turned on by different things, and sometimes you just can't get those yucky thoughts out of your head. They can even keep you up at night. For instance, noises, animals, dark places, scary stories, or bad dreams can turn on the switch. Thinking about monsters, bad guys, strangers, or being alone can scare us too. Some kids worry about going to the doctor, some kids worry about going to school, and some kids worry about people dying. Thunder, lightning, and stormy weather can be scary too. What things scare you?

Anxiety is like a message and we have to figure out when to pay attention to it. If we tell grown-ups when we feel afraid, they can even tell us whether it is the right time to worry or whether everything is really all right. They can help us figure out how to feel better.

Anxiety doesn't usually feel good, but sometimes it's a good thing, even though that's hard to believe. It's our body's way of telling us that we might be about to do something hard and it helps us get ready for the challenge. If we're going to have a test, it might remind us to study for it, or if we're going to be in a play, it tells us to practice our part so we feel ready. Those are times when anxiety is helpful.

But if we have too much anxiety, or it happens when we don't have a real challenge to get ready for, we might feel nervous or worried or really, really scared. We feel like something bad is going to happen. Our emergency switch is on and it's not supposed to be. We need to help it turn off so the anxiety won't get more powerful and make us feel worse and worse. Lots of people feel anxiety at different times and for different reasons. If we feel it a lot, chances are that other people in our family do too, even if we can't tell.

When the switch goes on and we want to make it go off, there are some things we can do to get rid of the anxiety. Everybody will have a way that he or she likes best. One thing we can do is breathe more slowly on purpose. If you breathe in air only through your nose, and blow it out very slowly from just your mouth, you will feel calmer. You can practice holding up a tissue in front of your face and watch it fly up as you breathe out slowly (count to five!) to make your breath last long. You can also try to blow a giant soap bubble through a wand very slowly and very carefully so it doesn't pop. Or blow into a harmonica, recorder, or kazoo softly and see how long you can make the sound last. If your heart feels fast and fluttery, you can cough very hard and that may also help to get it back on track.

Scientists found out that if you make yourself smile, your brain will make a happy chemical called serotonin (ser-uh-toh'-nin), and that makes us feel good. But if you just don't feel like smiling, try this trick. Put a clean pencil or chopstick in your mouth so both ends stick out from either side. Now, try biting down on the pencil with your back teeth. Since your lips won't close, they will automatically turn up into a smile, and this will make your brain think you are calm and happy. Hold that silly position for about one minute and your brain will start to lower your anxiety. Cool, huh?

You can also run around very fast, do jumping jacks, ride your bike, play a hopping game, or jump rope, and when you stop, your heart will slow down automatically and your body will feel better. Or, you can find something different to do that will distract you. Why not daydream about something fun? Change what you're doing or go somewhere else. You can sing out loud, turn on the radio, or watch TV. Try putting a rubber band around your wrist, and gently snap it when your thoughts start racing. Some people like to eat or drink something cold or hot, chocolaty, minty, or spicy to help their bodies feel the change.

If you have a tape or recording that teaches you how to relax the muscles in your body, you can listen to that and practice. Some people do yoga to help them learn how to breathe a better way. Yoga is a combination of exercise, concentration, breathing, and relaxation. Some kids like to pet a stuffed animal, take a warm bath, or smell something that reminds them of things they like. Other children like to catch their worries in a worry doll or dream catcher, or take a broom and sweep all bad ideas out of their rooms. And other kids like to be wrapped up all snuggly in bed or hugged very tight when they feel scared.

If your thoughts are still running away with you, picture this in your brain. Imagine you are walking down a road with this big old Worry Walrus. He magically appears wherever you are and he wants to weigh you down with the weight of his worries. The more he worries, the bigger he gets, and that makes him even more worried! He can't hurt you, and since he's especially happy to have company with him, he takes you along and fills you with ideas that make you wallow in your worries too. Okay, now, let's pretend that you are waiting for your mom to pick you up from school and the bell rang five minutes ago, but she isn't there yet.

Worry Walrus starts to pull you faster and faster down the road when suddenly you see it splits off into several paths. You have to choose which one to take. One road scares you because it sends the message, "She must have been in an accident!" Another sign freaks you out because it makes you wonder whether she got kidnapped. And another sign says, "Come and suffer down this road. She'll probably never show up!" Then, suddenly, you feel your emergency switch flipping. Well, what should do you? Here's the answer.

Stop! Don't go down those roads! Quick, close the gate! Act like a GPS and "recalculate." Choose another path. You can *definitely* think of other really good reasons why she might be late.

Talking with someone who makes you feel safe about what worries you will almost always make you feel better. In fact, if you can think about those worries in silly ways that might even make you laugh, they will actually lose their power. Like imagining a monster with hiccups or wearing a diaper and talking baby talk. You can also slow down all the worries in your brain by finding a different good reason to explain why you felt scared in the first place. Try talking yourself out of it.

Since you have a good brain, you can tell yourself messages inside your head that will help you to feel better. You've been scared before, and you've gotten over it. You can do it again. The idea is to outsmart your body when it tries to play a trick on you. Special people called psychologists, psychiatrists, and social workers are very good at showing you different ways to feel better. And sometimes your family and a doctor might decide together that vitamins or medicine is a good idea. If you can calm down faster when you get scared, then you will change the way your amygdala works so it doesn't send emergency messages to your body when it's not a real emergency.

We don't want that emergency switch to go on without a good reason. Remember, you are not a dinosaur and there usually isn't *real* danger. We all feel better if we can control when the emergency switch goes on, instead of feeling scared all the time. Grown-ups at home and at school will help keep you safe. It's okay to let them do the worrying instead, so you won't have to. If you don't feel safe, tell someone you trust, so you can work on changing things in order to feel better.

The job of children is to learn and to play, and the job of grownups is to take care of them and protect them. You'll be better at both of them if you don't worry when you don't have to. Find the things that make you feel better and maybe even invent some of your own. Grown-ups who love you want you to feel safe and calm and happy. And you will when you learn to control your own switch.

You can train your brain! Here are some rhymes to help you remember the ideas you just heard in this book.

TALK or WALK!

➡ helps you remember that you can talk to a grownup you trust. You can also change where you are and walk to another place. If you're inside, then go outside, or the other way around.

BLOW SLOW!

➡ helps you remember how to breathe to calm down.

SMILE FOR A WHILE

→ Even if you force yourself to smile, it will tell your brain to make the happy chemical, serotonin, that will help you feel calm.

RELAX – JUMPING JACKS!

→ helps you remember you can relax your body by listening to a special CD *or* doing yoga or you can speed it up by being active so your body will calm down by itself when you stop exercising.

DISTRACT – GET the FACT!

→ helps you remember that you can distract yourself and change what you're doing. **Get the fact** means that you can find a different **good** reason to explain what scared you instead of letting your imagination make something up.

DON'T WAIT—CLOSE THE GATE! TURN AROUND, RECALCULATE!

→ If your bad thoughts keep going down the same path, then STOP! Close the gate and choose another road. You can make a better choice.

Next time you read this book, you'll figure out which ideas you like the best. With a little bit of practice, you will be able to turn off your own emergency switch. You can train your brain to help you feel better and worry less. You really can!

Note to parents:

Fear, worry, and anxiety are normal occurrences within the life of a child. Helping children to understand and process these emotions often falls in the hands of parents, who by their own admission often feel painfully concerned, overwhelmed and unprepared to deal with these kinds of feelings. The only prototypes available to most families are those carried forward from generation to generation, with little information regarding the physiological and psychological facts surrounding anxiety, and even less regard for what children are feeling and thinking in the face of these emotions. Stomach aches, increased crying, refusal to go to school, irritability, changes in toileting habits, sleeplessness and nightmares, tics, eating too little or too much, increased need to sleep with parents, inattentiveness in school, preoccupation with negative thoughts, insatiable needs for reassurance, clinginess, increased startle responses, separation issues, self imposed isolation, repetitive behaviors and sadness can all be indicators of anxiety and worry in a child. How hard is it for a parent to remain calm and understanding in the face of their own child's fears, especially if they are unprepared and unsure of what to say? Becoming alarmed in the face of these behaviors and changes can only exacerbate the situation, and will certainly not do much to calm a child's fears.

In this book, Dr. Laurie Zelinger and our son, Jordan make every effort to provide families with a description of anxiety that children can understand, and suggestions that parents can use when addressing their child's concerns. Reading and ***re-reading*** this book with children will demystify anxiety, and provide families with the understanding needed to manage these uncomfortable emotions.

Parents must become aware of the difference between typical feelings of anxiety, and those that represent a more serious "mental health" concern. The simplest rules of thumb are based on frequency, impact upon regular life functions, persistence, and a pervasive sense of either hopelessness or worry. Many issues and transitions in the life a child are expected to cause temporary anxiety. When a developmentally common worry appears to get out of hand however, or stressors remain chronic, then contact with a licensed mental health professional is by all means indicated. Your pediatrician, the American Psychological Association or the Association for Play Therapy are among the resources that can help you find family support in your area.

Fred Zelinger, PhD
Licensed Psychologist

About the Author

Dr. Laurie Zelinger earned a Doctoral degree in psychology from Hofstra University on Long Island, New York and then went on to earn her credentials as a Registered Play Therapist/ Supervisor from the Association for Play Therapy. She is also a media specialist for the American Psychological Association and is frequently consulted on issues relating to childhood development. She and her psychologist husband, Dr. Fred Zelinger, have raised four sons. As a certified school psychologist, private practice licensed psychologist, and registered play therapist/supervisor, Dr. Laurie is treating increasing numbers of children with anxiety. She believes that honest and correct information, given at a child's developmental level in "kid-friendly" language, will help a youngster understand the link between body and feelings, the first step in symptom relief. Learn more about her and her other books at www.DrZelinger.com.

Jordan Zelinger is completing his doctoral degree in School-Clinical Child Psychology at Pace University in New York City. Jordan enjoys working with typically developing children and adolescents as well as those with special needs. He collaborated with his mother on this, his first book, drawing upon his background in psychology and undergraduate training in neuroscience. Jordan hopes to apply his skills in community mental health and school settings, as he begins to embark upon his professional career.

About the Illustrator

Elisa Sabella is a graduate of Rhode Island School of Design, where she earned a Bachelor of Fine Arts in Illustration. She currently works in New York as a cake decorator and spends her free time drawing and playing with her two ferrets. This is her first book.

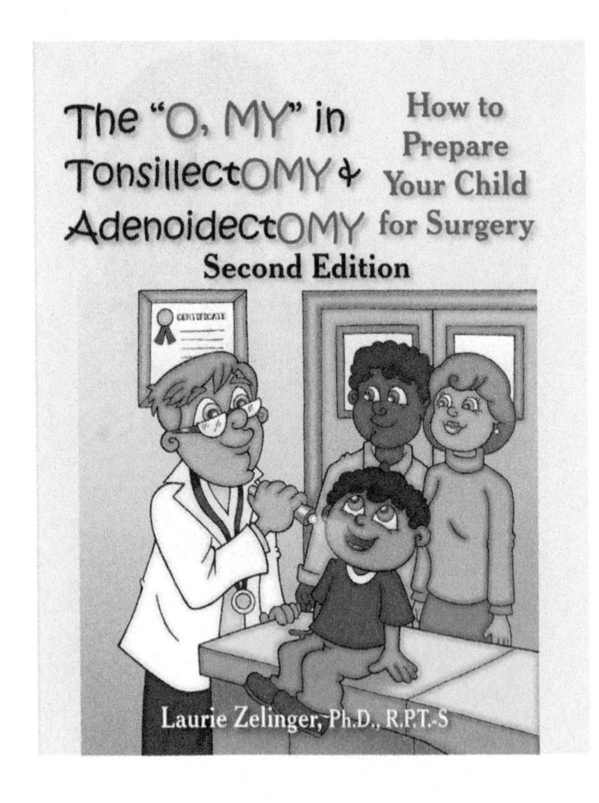

More than 200,000 tonsillectomies and adenoidectomies will be performed on children this year.

Will you be ready?

The new 2nd Edition of this bestselling book helps parents understand and organize the necessary medical and emotional components that accompany their child's surgery. In an easy to follow timeline for events prior to and following a tonsillectomy or adenoidectomy, the author provides reassuring and accurate guidance that eases the process for the patient and family.

Parents with this book will:

- Get the facts about tonsils and adenoids in simple terms
- Reduce your own anxiety about surgery
- Learn how to support your child through the medical and emotional events surrounding the procedure
- Take away the mystery regarding what to say to your child
- Discover the sequence of events leading up to surgery and how to prepare for them.
- Find out what you need to have at home while your child recuperates
- Become confident in knowing that you have maximized your child's comfort and adjustment during the weeks surrounding surgery
- Recognize symptoms of possible complications and take action

Professionals and Parents Praise Laurie Zelinger's Tonsillectomy Book:

"In over 40 years as a practicing Pediatrician, this is the most practical, down to earth and informative approach to the impending parent-child-hospital experience with a T&A that has come to my attention."
—Philip S. Steinfeld, MD, FAAP

"My son's recovery period was enhanced by advice from the manual, and thanks to Dr. Laurie, the bonding experience it created almost cancelled out the discomfort. He is now a strep-free, healthy boy! "
—Rachayle Salzberg (parent)

"...a valuable guide for parents intending to provide emotional preparation and support to a child about to undergo a surgical procedure. "
—Richard H. Wexler, PhD President, New York State Psychological Association (2008)

"This book is a great tool to help you understand what will be happening to your child, why they are performing the surgery, and what you need to know to be better prepared in caring for your child after the surgery is performed "
—Danielle Drake for *Reader Views*

The Growing With Love Series

Cinderella's Magical Wheelchair: An Empowering Fairy Tale

What Do You Use to Help Your Body? Maggie Explores the World of Disabilities

Cyber Bullying No More

Adopting a Child with a Trauma & Attachment Disruption History

CPSIA information can be obtained
at www.ICGtesting.com
Printed in the USA
BVOW07s1341281216
472038BV00007B/99/P

9 781615 992164